Grayscale Ad...

Partner/Designer

Laura Kilgore
kilgore7098@gmail.com

cebook #lifeescapescoloringbooks
ttps://coloringbooksforadults.shop

This is a Life Escapes Grayscale Adult Coloring Book

Grayscale is very different than your childhood coloring books. Grayscale is preferred by those who wish to produce realistic results.

What our website has to offer:

ore great adult coloring books (PDF only)
ee Color guide zip file (download)
ow to color grayscale video tutorials
ownload and color our freebies

Flip Through Videos
Colored pages from customers and fans
What's Inside Flip Through Videos
Coloring Greeting Cards

Our books are available in paperback on Amazon

Our website (coloringbooksforadults.shop) offers digital download PDF book files only. Print them on your paper of choice. Print the entire book or a single page at a time.

While on our website, sign up for our monthly newsletter and get a discount code for 50% off your digital orders for life.

Look at the back pages in this book for some getting started ips, instructions for downloading your free color guide and info about Life Escapes Grayscale Designers

For Business inquiries not reguarding artwork
Contact Kimberly Hawthorne at life.escapes.series@gmail.com

ife Escapes Grayscale Adult Coloring Books   Nature Mash-Ups By Laura Kilgore & Kimberly Hawthorne

https://adultcoloringcommunity.com

Buy Digital

Life Escapes Grayscale Adult Coloring Books   Artist Kimberly Hawthorne   Nature Mash-Ups By Laura Kilgore & Kimberly Hawthorne

https://adultcoloringcommunity.com

https://adultcoloringcommunity.com

Buy Digital

ife Escapes Grayscale Adult Coloring Books

Nature Mash-Ups By Laura Kilgore & Kimberly Hawthorne

https://adultcoloringcommunity.com

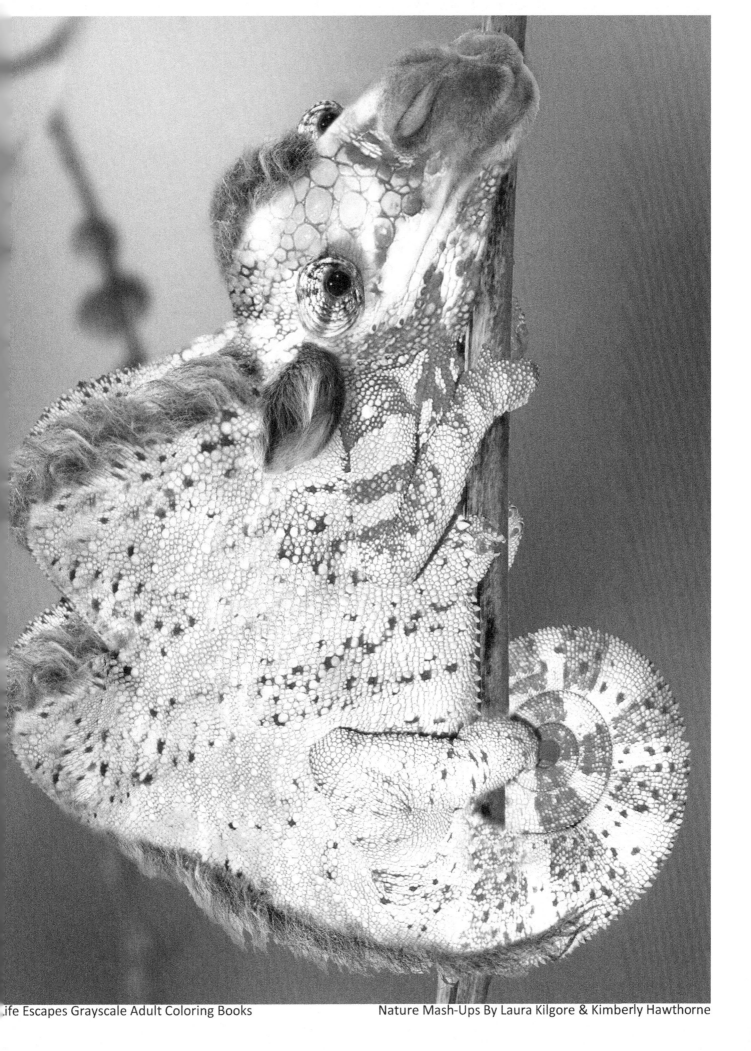

https://adultcoloringcommunity.com

https://adultcoloringcommunity.com

https://adultcoloringcommunity.com

Buy Digital

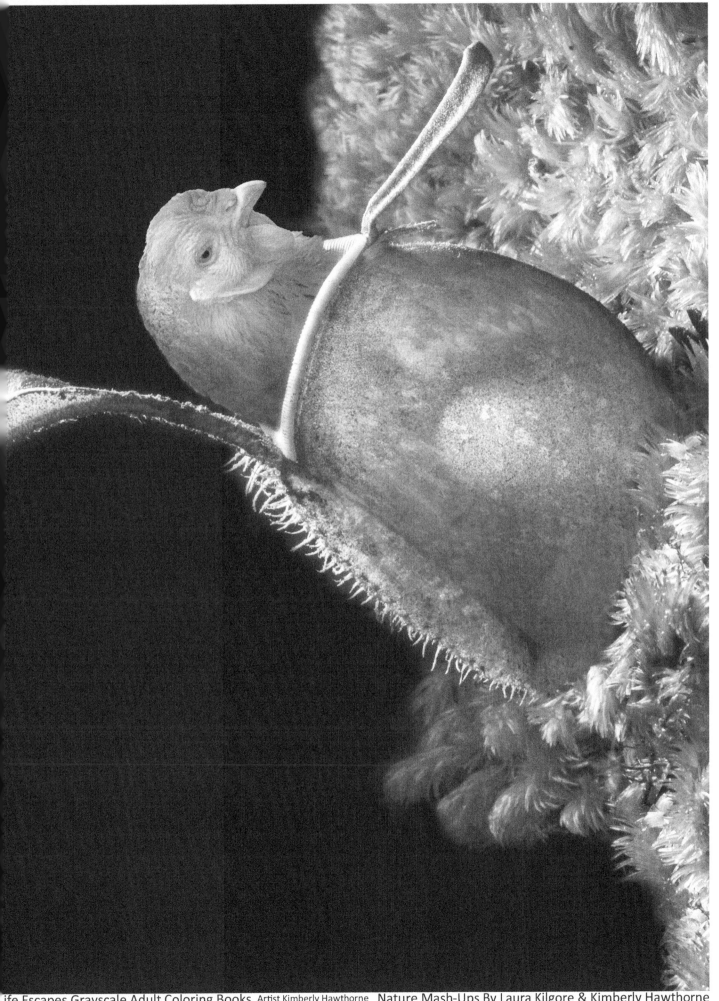

https://adultcoloringcommunity.com

https://adultcoloringcommunity.com

https://adultcoloringcommunity.com

https://adultcoloringcommunity.com	Buy Digital

https://adultcoloringcommunity.com

https://adultcoloringcommunity.com

https://adultcoloringcommunity.com

Buy Digital

https://adultcoloringcommunity.com

Buy Digital

Life Escapes Grayscale Adult Coloring Books — Artist Laura Kilgore — Nature Mash-Ups By Laura Kilgore & Kimberly Hawthorne

https://adultcoloringcommunity.com   Buy Digital

https://adultcoloringcommunity.com

https://adultcoloringcommunity.com

COLOR TEST PAGE

@Life Escapes Grayscale Adult Coloring Books

Nature Mash-Ups By Laura Kilgore & Kimberly Hawthorne

https://coloringbooksforadults.shop
How to get your FREE color guide

As of April 1, 2020 we no longer honor our free pdf with amazon purchase. You may continue to download the free color guide for all our books on our website. Here is how to do it.

1. Go to https://coloringbooksforadults.shop
2. Click on top menu button that says full pdf library
3. Find the cover pic of your book and click on it
4. Scroll down to the color guide section and click the button to download the color guide

Introducing...

How to color grayscale video tutorials for sale on our website.

Watch our Basics Series Free

Go to the site address at the top then click on the "How to Color Grayscale" button in the top menu

Still Need Help?
life.escapes.series@gmail.com

Basic Grayscale Coloring Instructions

Step 1 - Choose an object in the coloring page to start with then you will need black, white and light, medium & dark shades of the color you choose. (Examples: a tree, an animal, a flower etc...)

Step 2 - With your color pencils, coloring in a circular motion, color white and light gray areas with your light color. Color dark grays with your dark color. Color medium grays with your medium color.

Tip: Overlap medium color a little ways into the light and dark areas for a seamless blend of your colors.

Step 3 - If you color with a light hand, add more layers of color to make it more visible or vibrant. Then on the highlight areas, add white over the area. Use black to outline and enhance the very darkest areas.

Tip: Keep your pencils sharp and color in a circular motion. If you have a heavy hand, move your fingers higher up on the pencil to ensure you are coloring lightly when needed.

For further techniques, methods, mediums, tips and tricks, check out our all new video tutorials on our website.

Go to https://coloringbooksforadults.shop

Then click on "How to Color Grayscale" button in the top menu

Our videos on the basics are free to watch

We want you to enjoy your coloring experience

If you are struggling with an image, please go to http://coloringbooksforadults.shop to download the color guide for this book. You will also find videos on how to color grayscale. If you still need assistance, please email Kimberly at life.escapes.series@gmail.com

Follow us on Facebook @lifeescapescoloringbooks

Grayscale Adult Coloring Books
life.escapes.series@gmail.com
https://coloringbooksforadults.shop

More Great Books by Laura Kilgore

https://adultcoloringcommunity.com

Grayscale Adult Coloring Books

life.escapes.series@gmail.com

https://coloringbooksforadults.shop

More Great Books by Kimberly Hawthorne

@Life Escapes Grayscale Adult Coloring Books

Nature Mash-Ups By Laura Kilgore & Kimberly Hawthorne

Grayscale Adult Coloring Books
life.escapes.series@gmail.com
https://coloringbooksforadults.shop

More Great Books by Susan Mowery

  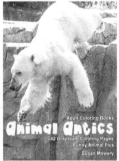   

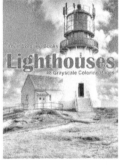   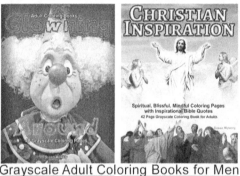  

Grayscale Adult Coloring Books for Men

 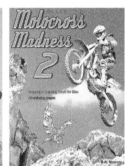    

     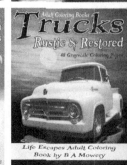

https://adultcoloringcommunity.com

Buy Digital

Grayscale Adult Coloring Books

life.escapes.series@gmail.com

https://coloringbooksforadults.shop

More Great Books by Timothy Parks

     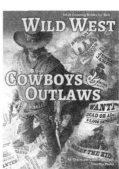

Grayscale Adult Coloring Books
life.escapes.series@gmail.com
https://coloringbooksforadults.shop

Life Escapes Popular Book Series'

Coming soon

Coming soon

Coming soon

Coming soon

https://adultcoloringcommunity.com

Grayscale Adult Coloring Books
life.escapes.series@gmail.com
https://coloringbooksforadults.shop

More Life Escapes Popular Book Series'

Coming soon

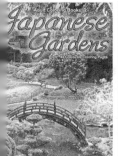 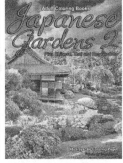   

End of Series

  Coming soon  Coming soon

  Coming soon   Coming soon

  Coming soon

@Life Escapes Grayscale Adult Coloring Books   Nature Mash-Ups By Laura Kilgore & Kimberly Hawthorne

Grayscale Adult Coloring Books
life.escapes.series@gmail.com
https://coloringbooksforadults.shop

More Life Escapes Popular Book Series'

  Coming soon  Coming soon

 Coming soon   Coming soon

  End of Series  Coming soon

  Coming soon   Coming soon

  Coming soon   Coming soon

https://adultcoloringcommunity.com

Buy Digital

NOTICE

Images used to create this coloring book have been compiled by Life Escapes grayscale designers. We do not take credit for the original artwork. We are credited for alterations and the method of our grayscaling of the original artwork.

The images used were legally compiled from sites and artists offering commercial use via free membership or paid membership. We cannot possibly know about and therefore cannot be responsible for unlawful images posted on those sites.

Some of our images sources - but not limited to...

Creative Commons	freedesignfile.com
Public Domain	vectorfree.com
Expired Copyright	vectoropenstock.com
Free for Commercial Use	pxhere.com
Vecteezy.com Premium Membership	freevector.com
Brusheezy.com Premium Membership	pngimage.com
all-free-download.com attribution	pngmart.com
Deviantart.com Commercial Use Ok	freepngimages.com
Dreamstime Premium Membership	freegreatpicture.com
Envato.com Premium Membership	pngpix.com
freepik.com Premium Membership	pixabay.com
Adobe Stock Photos Purchased	Unsplash.com
DepositPhotos Premium Member	wikimedia.commons.org
	freestockphotos.biz

Disclaimer: All original artwork provided digitally is protected via a watermark of Life Escapes logo. This watermark doesn't mean we claim credit for original artwork. It is to protect the original artists which are largely unknown to us. When we know who the original artist is, we place the info below the coloring page.

With that being said, we give our customers personal use rights to our grayscaled coloring pages.

Personal use means you can make copies of uncolored images/pages in print or digital format from this book for your own personal use, but you cannot distribute them in any way without written permission from Life Escapes Adult Coloring Books owner - Kimberly Hawthorne and/or partnering artists.
This license includes but is not limited to the following:
Any and all uncolored images/pages as they appear in print, pdf, digital download and on website (http://coloringbooksforadults.shop)
Exception: free coloring pages offered on website and social media can be shared freely online when linking back to any page on coloringbooksforadults.shop.
You may NOT share coupon codes or links for digital downloads.

To report an image

For questions, comments or other...please contact us at
life.escapes.series@gmail.com

Made in the USA
Monee, IL
01 October 2022